Masters of Modern Architecture

LE CORBUSIER

LE CORBUSIER

Introduction and notes by
MARTIN PAWLEY

with photographs by
YUKIO FUTAGAWA

96 illustrations, 11 in colour

THAMES AND HUDSON · LONDON

First published in Japan in 1967 by Bijutsu Shuppan-sha, Tokyo, in their series GENDAI KENCHIKUKA SHIRIZU.
New texts have been provided for this English language edition.

Printed in Japan

0 500 58004 9

Contents

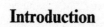

Introduction

Charles-Edouard Jeanneret was born at La Chaux-de-Fonds, Switzerland, on 6 October 1887. His father was an engraver and his mother a musician of some accomplishment: both were chiefly employed engraving the cases of locally made watches and clocks.

The fact that Le Corbusier (he adopted this name in 1920 under the influence of the painter Ozenfant, who himself had many pseudonyms) did not become widely known until the publication of *Vers une Architecture* in 1923, when he was 36 years old, has tended to obscure the importance of his career prior to the First World War—although it can be argued that the revelation of all that was to come later began as early as 1908. In that year he was living in France and working in the atelier of Auguste Perret, the celebrated pioneer in the use of reinforced concrete. Financed by a grant from La Chaux-de-Fonds School of Art, Jeanneret had already travelled in Italy and Germany, and had penetrated as far as Budapest and met Joseph Hoffmann (a seminal figure in Austrian modern architecture) in Vienna. Between 1906 and 1908 he had designed three houses, the Villas Fallet, Jacquemet and Stotzer, in his home town; and in a letter to his former teacher and benefactor, Professor Charles l'Eplattenier, he announced that he felt worthy of a career other than that of engraver, but that if he was to succeed as an architect in the manner which he now felt necessary it would require an enormous step forward, an effort of which he was only then beginning to be capable.

> '. . . aujourd'hui, c'est fini des petits rêves enfantins d'une réussite semblable à celle d'une ou deux écoles d'Allemagne, Vienne, Darmstadt.[1] C'est trop facile, et je veux me battre avec la vérité elle-même. Elle me martyrisera peut-être, sûrement. Ce n'est pas la quiétude, qu'aujourd'hui j'envisage et me prépare pour l'avenir. Et peut-être moins encore le triomphe de la foule. . . Mais moi, je vivrai—sincère—et de l'invective je serai heureux.'[2]

These bold and manifestly predictive words led l'Eplattenier to send the young Jeanneret once more to Germany to study the problems of decorative art, where for a short time he worked in the office of Peter Behrens, one of the first architects to devote his attention to the problems of industrial design.

Leaving Behrens in 1911, Jeanneret moved to Hellerau, near Dresden, and studied the activities of the *Deutscher Werkbund*—an organization founded in 1907 by leading artists, architects and designers with the aim of improving the quality of design of German manufactured goods. During his brief stay at Behrens' office, Jeanneret had met Walter Gropius and, by a matter of weeks, missed Mies van der Rohe, who had worked there before him.

Leaving Hellerau the young Swiss repaired again to Berlin only to leave shortly after on a seven-month tour of the Balkans in the entourage of August Klipstein, the wealthy Berlin antiquary. This excursion over, he returned to La Chaux-de-Fonds to take charge of a course at the school of art under l'Eplattenier. For five years he busied himself with teaching and painting, immune to the desperate struggle being fought out in France, Russia and the Middle East. In 1916 he designed and supervised the construction of the Villa Schwob, a building which later gained the admiration of the painter Ozenfant by virtue of its rigorously classic proportions and carefully executed detail in an otherwise suburban area.

In 1917 as a result of an obscure contract with the Voisin aircraft and automobile company, Jeanneret left Switzerland for Paris where he installed himself in a studio at 20 Rue Jacob—an address he was to retain for the next seventeen years. Shortly after his arrival in Paris Auguste Perret introduced him to Ozenfant and thus began an extraordinarily fruitful partnership which lasted till 1925. At this time Jeanneret considered himself a painter first and an architect second—largely as a result of the near impossibility of obtaining commissions during wartime. Nonetheless when his partnership with Ozenfant was solemnized in a railway carriage on the way to Andernos (where Ozenfant had a country retreat), special attention was devoted to the risk Jeanneret was running in promoting himself as a painter when the more serious profession of architect was his real ambition.[3] Their first exhibition, accompanied by a manifesto entitled 'Après le Cubisme', was dedicated to the advancement of 'Purism'—an artistic doctrine of pure geometry which they both espoused, believing that the overwhelming triumph of geometry, 'the thumb-print of modern technology',[4] represented a plateau in the evolution of design for both art and science. This belief led them, in association with the poet Paul Dermée and with irregular financial aid from Voisin and other industrialists, to found *L'Esprit Nouveau*, a magazine with a limited circulation dealing with architecture, painting, sculpture, industrial design, music, literature, philosophy, psychology, politics and economics.[5] The magazine ran from immediately after the 'Purist' exhibition of 1919 until 1925 when the partnership broke up.

The precise relationship between *L'Esprit Nouveau* and *Vers une Architecture*, and more particularly between Ozenfant and Jeanneret as to the matter of authorship, has yet to be clearly established. There is little doubt that the chapters of *Vers une Architecture* are reworked articles which originally appeared in *L'Esprit Nouveau*; there is also little doubt that the principal reason for the great popular success of *Vers une Architecture* was the wholly convincing nature of the *photographic evidence* which it contained. Many of Le Corbusier's later projects, particularly his houses, are to be seen clearly in the illustrations of promenade decks on liners, 'cubist' automobiles and biplane aircraft which crowd its pages. Further to this we have Ozenfant's own recollection[6] that shortly after he suggested to Jeanneret that he employ the name of a distant cousin—Lecorbesier—in the form 'Le Corbusier' ('en deux sections, cela fera plus riche!') as a pseudonym, they developed a pattern of working whereby 'j'avais apporté les illustrations, il avait rédigé les commentaires.' From this circumstantial evidence, allied to Ozenfant's displeasure at the reception accorded to *Vers une Architecture* and the collapse of their partnership shortly afterwards, it seems all too possible that 'Lecorbesier' derived at least some of his astonishing insights into the qualities inherent in the design of ships, cars, aircraft and briar pipes from the serendipitous Ozenfant. The chapter in *Vers une Architecture* which features the North American grain silos originally appeared in *L'Esprit Nouveau* in October 1920, when it was signed 'Le Corbusier-Saugnier' (which is to say Jeanneret-Ozenfant) as the result of an agreement whereby articles on painting were to be signed first by Ozenfant, and those on architecture signed first by Jeanneret.

These fine distinctions, whose real importance will be clear only to those who have involved themselves at one time or another in the world of little magazines, reveals something of the precarious life-style of the young Corbusier in the 1920s. Rather more has been unearthed by Reyner Banham, an architectural writer and historian with an uncanny capacity for unravelling the bombastic utterances of the avant garde. Using the chapter in *Vers une Architecture* dealing with the practical requirements of the dwelling, which contains a list of 'demands' earlier adumbrated by a certain 'Dr Winter' (another alias) in *L'Esprit Nouveau*, Banham suggests that

'. . . hardly any of these demands were satisfied in the houses that Le Corbusier designed in the years succeeding this pronouncement of 1921. He did not build any of them until the beginning of 1923, so none of these propositions are based upon recent constructional experience. They are, rather, based upon recent experience of living in rented accommodation in Paris ("Demand of your landlord . . . etc.") and addressed to young intellectuals in a similar position to himself. It is less a manual of housing than a manifesto on converted property rules for making oneself comfortable in the *quartier Latin*.'[7]

Le Corbusier only really emerged from this twilight world of manifestos, bravado, uncertain authorship and rented rooms when the publicity resulting from the success of *Vers une Architecture* began to bring in its train commissions from outside the wealthy café-society of Paris. In the meantime he had a steady trickle of small jobs to contend with, each of which could in some small way serve as a dry-run for part of the general theory of urbanism which he developed throughout the period of *L'Esprit Nouveau*. A good example of this process occurred when the International Exhibition of Decorative Arts of 1925, for which he designed the pavilion 'Esprit Nouveau', served as the 'site' for one unit of his Villa-Apartment project of 1922. This project featured apartments arranged in a four-storey block so that each possessed a terrace-garden penetrating the entire width of the block in the manner of a brick honeycomb wall. The exhibition pavilion—apart from a tree which stood on the site and penetrated the roof of the garden area—was worked up from the design drawings of an individual unit in the 120-apartment block.

Projects could also generate bigger projects in the same way. The 'town of three million inhabitants', a skyscraper project featuring serried ranks of cruciform tower blocks set in a rigid grid of lower buildings, which was published in the last issue of *L'Esprit Nouveau* in January 1925, formed the basis for the later 'Plan Voisin' for Paris which was shown at the same exhibition as the pavilion 'Esprit Nouveau'. Both these projects in turn contributed to the 'Ville Radieuse' project of 1930, the 'Ilôt insalubre' slum-clearance project of 1936, and eventually to the Berlin redevelopment plan of 1958. The evolution of Le Corbusier's 'Citrohan' house designs followed a similar linear path with each successive project making use of what went before. This principle is not unknown in journalism where it is called 'making every shot count twice': it speaks more eloquently than do the architect's later words of the endless delays and opposition with which he had to contend before he was finally entrusted with commissions equal to his ambition.

The first development which could be said to fall into this category was the commission to construct a large number of concrete houses at Pessac near Bordeaux for the wealthy industrialist Henri Frugès in 1925. Prior to this date the Ozenfant house of 1922, the Villa Vaucresson of the same year, and the Villa La Roche of 1925 had only allowed 'one-off' exploration of the possibilities inherent in free-form plans, roof gardens, *pilotis* and full-width window bands. At Pessac Frugès announced that he wanted the site to become a laboratory for the development of Le Corbusier's ideas on mass-production:

> 'I am going to enable you to realise your theories in practice—right up to their most extreme consequences—Pessac shall be a laboratory. In short: I ask you to pose the problem of a house plan, of finding a method of standardisation, to make use of walls, floors and roofs conforming to the most rigorous requirements for strength and efficiency and lending themselves to true Taylor-like methods of mass production by the use of machines which I will authorise you to buy.'

This noble offer, recounted in the above form by Le Corbusier[8] but recollected rather differently by Frugès himself,[9] proved to be the prelude to a sequence of disasters and disappointments culminating in the refusal of the Bordeaux authorities to grant permits of habitation to the forty houses which were eventually completed out of the proposed two hundred. Alarmed at the turn events had taken, Frugès proposed that the houses should be painted on the outside to render them more attractive to potential purchasers. Most unwillingly Le Corbusier complied, producing a unique arrangement of painted projections and reveals using bright colours—a chance departure which was later to become, in the 'Unités' and at Chandigarh, almost the architect's trademark.

Following the partial failure of this ambitious enterprise Le Corbusier returned to the construction of villas for the rich and very rich. The Villa Cook, built at Boulogne in 1926, embodied all the elements experimented with at Pessac without the embarrassing necessity for wholly premature attempts at mass-production. Here there are *pilotis* to lift the building clear of the landscape, a roof-garden to 'replace' the site area used, a free internal plan and wide strips of window with sliding sashes. The same basic ideas were incorporated in the following year into the two houses the architect designed for the second International Exposition of the *Deutscher Werkbund* at Stuttgart in Germany. This Exposition, which took the form of a model suburb—the Weissenhofsiedlung —built at great expense on the outskirts of the city, was composed of architectural contributions from almost all the well-known modern architects of Europe. Mies van der Rohe was himself in charge of the distribution of commissions. Le Corbusier's two houses stood next to an apartment block by Mies and houses by Oud, Gropius, Hilberseimer, Bruno Taut, Poelzig, Behrens and Hans Scharoun. Le Corbusier's own designs, one a 'Citrohan' (mass-production prototype) house arrived at after ten years of design study, and the other an open-planned apartment house with movable partitions which could close off private areas if necessary, were accompanied by the publication of the architect's famous 'five points of modern architecture.'

These 'five points'—the replacement of cellars and foundations by piles and *pilotis*; the use of roof gardens; the point loading of floor supports to free internal planning; the change from windows to strips of glass ('repetitive mechanical elements') running from wall to wall, and thus—logically—the creation of a curtain-wall façade which would no longer carry load. All these elements had been present in Le Corbusier's work from 1923 onwards, but by 1929 they had become increasingly assured in their relationship with one another. The large villa at Carthage, Tunisia, which the architect built in that year was arguably his first mature work in the sense of an apparently effortless combination of design concepts scarcely five years old in theory, let alone practice. Despite his preoccupation with industrialized housing—he continued to experiment with Prouvé throughout the 1930s—Le Corbusier was now entering a definitive phase in his career as an architect with an increasing emphasis on expensive private villas and urban structure. Low-cost, low-density housing of the kind exemplified at Pessac seemed to interest him less as he grew older—at Chandigarh in 1950 he turned large areas of housing over to collaborators and concentrated instead on the prestige public buildings of the capitol.

Le Corbusier's reputation still rested largely on his book *Vers une Architecture*; in a worsening economic and political climate his efforts to secure large commissions had almost all failed—the one exception was the Centrosoyus office building in Moscow for which working drawings were delivered but supervision of construction was denied. The competition for a Palace of the League of Nations at Geneva held in 1927 had ended in lawsuits and bitterness, all directly attributable to the pusillanimity of the jury who awarded nine first prizes instead of resolving their own disputes over traditional versus modern design— with the result that the commission was later awarded to an *ad hoc* group of four traditional architects who took a further two years to produce a workable though mediocre scheme.

Nonetheless the same period saw the construction of the Salvation Army Headquarters in Paris and the commissioning of two of the architect's most admired works: the Pavillon Suisse, the Swiss Pavilion at the Cité Universitaire, Paris; and 'Les Heures Claires', his finest large house, at Poissy (1931). The first of these buildings, the Salvation Army Headquarters, enabled Le Corbusier to experiment for the first time[10] with his own conception of air conditioning, a 'closed' system which recirculated air via a 'ventilation plant where chemical baths remove the carbon dioxide and it then goes on to be regenerated in an ozonifier, and into coolers if it has been overheated.'[11] A scheme of this kind has been detailed for the Centrosoyus office building and despatched to Moscow with the plans, but for reasons which Le Corbusier liked to describe as technical unsophistication it was not incorporated into the office complex when it was built. As Banham notes, it is with astonishment that one realises Le Corbusier really did mean a recirculating system of ventilation as used today in nuclear submarines and spacecraft.

> 'Arguing narrowly from first principles he had come up with another of his stunningly crude and absolute solutions, unreal and unworkable, to an entirely real problem. Willis Carrier [the American inventor of air-conditioning] had long before arrived at solutions more subtle, economical, flexible and practical, of which Le Corbusier appears to have been totally ignorant—he seems never to have used the words "air conditioning" or their French equivalents, until after his first visit to the USA in 1935–1936.'[12]

The failure of Le Corbusier's invention of the *mur neutralisant* (a system of double glazing with warm air circulating between the two layers of glass) in the Salvation Army building largely derived from cost limitations which at the last minute prevented the 'ventilation plant' from being installed. Instead the intrepid architect went ahead with only a single sealed skin of glass on the south wall of the dormitory block. At the opening in December 1933 this expedient worked well, with many visitors commenting on the tropical atmosphere; unfortunately in the summer of the following year opinions had changed and the city authorities of Paris insisted on the insertion of opening lights. This problem in one form or another was to haunt Le Corbusier for most of his professional life; for reasons of pride or economy he hardly ever employed air conditioning, and his own answer—the *brise soleil*—was, as Banham observes, an example of the process by which the advantages of the traditional massive wall (which Le Corbusier had banished with his 'five points of modern architecture') were argued back one at a time. The Salvation Army building itself, badly damaged during the Second World War, was fitted with *brise soleil* afterwards by Le Corbusier's cousin Pierre Jeanneret.

Another serious defect of the light frame construction advocated by Le Corbusier was brought into prominence by the poor acoustic performance of the Swiss Pavilion. This commission, offered to the architect by an organization of the Swiss universities as compensation for the disgraceful mishandling of the League of Nations competition, featured study-bedrooms separated by non-structural walls on the upper floors. Here Le Corbusier carried out experiments using suspended lead sheets in the light-weight partitions, but to little avail for the building is still renowned for its poor sound reduction. The architect once again pleaded lack of money—the budget being reduced by one half—but the conducting of experiments in sound insulation is hardly the hallmark of a cheap building, then or now. Apart from its poor environmental performance, the Swiss Pavilion was an enormous success amongst the small group of admirers of modern architecture at the time. In contradistinction to the Salvation Army building and to some of the architect's earlier projects, it was probably the first of his 'timeless' designs

—conceptions which seem neither to belong to the particular date at which they were built nor to any other time. The massive *pilotis* and carefully articulated slab blocks of the Pavilion foreshadow the massive structures of the architect's post-war work, in fact they represent the brief confluence of two generations of ideas: the glass wall which stems fundamentally from the Domino house projects of 1914–16, and the massive *in-situ* concrete structure which was to make its first clear appearance in the Algerian skyscraper project of 1938–39.

Just prior to the completion of the Swiss Pavilion came the topping out of 'Les Heures Claires', the Villa Savoye at Poissy. This house marks the point at which Le Corbusier graduated from *enfant terrible* to old master at the age of forty-two. 'Les Heures Claires' consists of a square box of reinforced concrete supported on a dozen round concrete *pilotis*. Deeply recessed under this concrete box are an entrance hall and a garage. The entire ensemble is sited between groups of trees in a flat area of *pelouse*. Peter Blake wrote of this house:

'The precise geometric silhouette of the Villa Savoye permitted no confusion of architecture with nature. This was meant to be a man-made object, the product of man's one great distinguishing characteristic—pure reason. . .   The second floor patio, upon which all the living spaces are centred, is a real garden: a paved courtyard with carefully controlled planting in boxes. Moreover, the views of the surrounding fields and trees are just as carefully controlled: on all four sides of the concrete box there are horizontal viewing slots through which sections of the landscape appear like naturalistic murals painted, between pilasters, in some great room of a Renaissance Palace. Only the roof of this patio, this outdoor room, is entirely open—to the sky.'[13]

'Les Heures Claires' enjoyed only a few years of domestic use. Its owners fled before the advancing Germans in 1940 and the building itself deteriorated rapidly during the war. In 1959 the development of neighbouring areas threatened its destruction until, at the instigation of André Malraux, it was renovated and now stands—surrounded by buildings—intact but shorn of its former glory.

The 1930s were not a happy time for Le Corbusier. The Congrès International d'Architecture Moderne (CIAM), an organization founded by the architect, Siegfried Giedion (the Swiss art-historian), and other leading architects of the modern movement in the aftermath of the League of Nations fiasco, failed to achieve the much needed popular breakthrough, and the monotonous succession of competition entries declared *hors de concours* or rejected without explanation continued. Among them was the large project for a Palace of the Soviets in Moscow, which featured an enormous parabolic arch supporting the roof of an assembly hall capable of seating 6,500 persons. From this period also dates the revolutionary 'Project Shrapnel' (so called because of the shell-burst effect it was supposed to have upon an astonished world) for a complete reorganization of the city of Algiers. This plan, first published in 1934, created an image of superbly organized urbanism whose effect upon the architectural profession is not yet exhausted. 'Project Shrapnel' established a new scale for the apartment block, and by rejecting the rigid symmetry of earlier schemes gained support from quarters previously resistant to Le Corbusier's ideas. One of the most astonishing features of this plan was the linking of two of the most widely separated suburbs of Algiers by means of an elevated expressway whose concrete support structure doubles as a matrix for apartments housing 180,000 persons. The sinuous curves of the new residential area proposed in the plan were to reappear in numerous projects afterwards, notably in South America—where much notice was taken of Le Corbusier's work—and even in Britain where twenty-five years later the Hyde Park central area redevelopment in Leeds was based upon the design of 'Project Shrapnel'.

With the passing of the conviction that machine production, geometry and rip-roaring urbanism were the 'inevitable' solution to the environmental problems of the cities of the West, Le Corbusier began to some extent to abdicate the position he had adopted in 1923. In Germany the Weimar Republic, whose encouragement of modern design particularly in architecture had been an inspiration to Le Corbusier's contemporaries, had passed away and the new Nazi régime was concentrating on ideas diametrically opposed to the kind of urbanism which the architect had long advocated. In France the steady slide towards defeat had begun with a succession of ineffective governments and a generally reactionary attitude towards design. Czechoslovakia, where Mies van der Rohe had built the Tugendhat house—one of the canonical buildings of the modern movement—at Brno, was about to suffer dissection at the hands of the invading Germans. Italy, ruled by the Fascist Mussolini since 1922, had witnessed the decline of modern idealism into neoclassic officialese. In Britain only a sprinkling of modern villas proclaimed the presence of an 'esprit nouveau'. Worse still, the architect's first visit to America in 1935 revealed possible loopholes in his earlier image of skyscraper living. For a start the question of land values was obviously something he had never understood. The 'Ville Radieuse' project demanded densities of 400 persons per acre with the population housed in superblocks, thus leaving 88% of the site area free for parkland; yet in Manhattan and parts of Los Angeles densities of this order —which seemed phenomenal in Europe—had already been achieved several times over. Radio City and the Empire State building both operated during working hours to densities of over 10,000 persons per acre, but there was no question of leaving 88% of the land open, or even 8%: the cost of doing so would have ruined the already risky economics of building so high in the first place. Without rigorous city planning—which is to say without complete control over land use—the skyscraper was no more a tool of enlightenment than was the automobile an unrelieved blessing. In a letter to the editor of *American Architect*[14] Le Corbusier wrote:

'Manhattan is so antagonistic to the fundamental needs of the human heart that the one idea of everybody is to escape. To get out. To avoid wasting one's own life and that of one's family in that hard, implacable atmosphere. To see the sky. To live where there are trees and to look out on grass. To escape forever from the noise and racket of the city.'

On his return to France Le Corbusier concentrated increasingly on the use of the simplest materials; timber, stone, concrete, brick and quarry tiles. The Mandrot house of 1932 and the later summer house at Mathes had already shown drift in this direction; allied to the architect's new conviction that large units of accommodation set in open parkland were the solution to urban living, this general tendency established the course of his post-war career. His disappointment in the American skyscraper also played a part in this process of synthesis and both the 'Cartesian' skyscraper of 1938, with its 'Y' shaped plan-form, and the even more sophisticated lozenge-shaped tower for the 'quartier de la Marine' in Algiers betrayed a new concern with some of the real problems of high-rise construction. The seventeen-storey Ministry of Education and Health in Rio de Janeiro, designed in the late 1930s in collaboration with Oscar Niemeyer and completed in 1945, brought together in a more successful combination many of the techniques of environmental control Le Corbusier had developed since the fiasco of the Salvation Army building in Paris.

With the fall of France in May 1940 Le Corbusier (then aged 52) retired to the South and began to try to interest the Vichy government in plans for large-scale reconstruction. With the occupation of Vichy in 1942 he reverted to painting and began work on the 'Modulor', a system of proportional rather than incremental modular measurements which would, in the words of Einstein—to whom the architect showed his work in 1946—'make the bad difficult and the good easy.' After the liberation of Paris he returned to the capital. Here he entertained visiting architects and students from abroad, supervised the repair of some of his more seriously damaged buildings and began work on two major projects: a new city plan for the Vosges town of Saint-Dié which had been almost entirely destroyed during the war; and the projected construction of four 350-apartment *Unités d'habitation*, on either side of the Boulevard Michelet at Marseilles, to rehouse the inhabitants of the destroyed Vieux-Port area. Of these plans the first came to nothing although the city centre designed was used as the starting point for the capitol at Chandigarh in India five years later. The Marseilles project, which succeeded in capturing the attention of the French Minister of Reconstruction, M. Claudius-Petit, was finally commissioned in 1947 and completed in 1952. During the course of construction the programme was reduced from four *Unités* to one, which was built to the east of the Boulevard Michelet between Vieux-Port and Marseille-Veyre.

This large building, notwithstanding its close relationship to some of Le Corbusier's urban projects of the 1920s, represents for the first time the architect's answer to the problems of construction cost, land value, maintenance and sheer practicability. Publicly financed, the *Unité* had to be cheap, and rehousing poor people—at least in intention, for the seven-year gestation period ensured that most of the original homeless had found alternative accommodation by 1952—it had to represent an economic use of land; built during a period of austerity and recovery, it could not make use of sophisticated and expensive materials. Completed under a hail of criticism and prejudice, the *Unité* was *obliged* to represent some kind of breakthrough in housing—for the sake of the government as much as the architect.

In a sense it achieved all these things: it was not cheap, largely as a result of delays and objections which were not directly attributable to the design, but it was popular. Two later *Unités*, at Nantes-Rezé and Berlin, were both *requested* by the people who would use them (Nantes), or the authority which was to pay (Berlin). Like his incomparable pre-war villas, the *Unités d'habitation* represented a sort of popular success in a way that the architect's numerous urban projects failed to do throughout the whole of his life. Chandigarh, the apparent exception to this rule, was in no sense a piece of urbanism in the tradition of the 'Ville Radieuse'. It was projected as an extremely horizontal, low-density garden city, perhaps as a result of the prejudices of predominantly English-educated Indian government officials with whom Le Corbusier negotiated the master plan between 1950 and 1952.

The increasing number of commissions from overseas, particularly from developing countries, which came Le Corbusier's way after 1950 reflected in great measure the truth of the old adage that the prophet lacks honour only in his own country. Since the early 1920s the architect had been an inveterate pamphleteer, proselytiser and propagandist for his own ideas. CIAM, the organization whose effect in the pre-war decade had appeared to be negligible, had in fact influenced a number of key teachers whose post-war positions in schools of architecture all over the world helped produce a whole generation of graduates brought up on *Vers une Architecture, Concerning Town Planning*, and the 'Athens Charter' of CIAM. These young men who appeared at Le Corbusier's atelier in the Rue de Sèvres in greater numbers than ever before hailed from the four corners of the earth. They were often related to influential politicians or industrialists in their own countries, and many of them rose to positions of high administrative power on their return from training in the universities of Europe and America. Viewed in this light it is less surprising that the major works of Le Corbusier's last decade were carried out in India, where partition and independence had created enormous planning and administrative problems. Le Corbusier's work at Chandigarh and Ahmedabad stems directly from this situation.

His career took one further novel step when at the age of 63 he accepted a commission to build a new chapel at Ronchamp in the Vosges mountains to replace an earlier building bombed during the war. The structure which emerged in 1953 was as radically different from the 'Cartesian' quality of his pre-war work as was the rough-cast concrete of the Chandigarh capitol buildings from the smooth 'pan de verre' façades of the apartment blocks of 'La Ville Radieuse'. Here, as at Marseilles, he achieved a timeless, style-less piece of architecture which Peter Blake describes as follows:

> 'The great curved masses of Ronchamp might be the result of acoustic determination, as Corbu declared; but they formed, together with the deep, irregularly spaced slot windows in the walls, a mysterious aura that was as reminiscent of the catacombs or the massive stone monasteries of the middle ages as it was of some dimly understood spatial concepts of today and tomorrow.'[15]

'Modulor' and pure sculptural ability combined to produce an enormous *succès d'estime* which led in time to the commission for the Dominican monastery of La Tourette and to the projected frustum-shaped Eglise de Firminy, construction of which had not begun at the time of Le Corbusier's death in 1965. The early 1960s saw Le Corbusier with more current commissions than at any time in his life, yet in this belated acceptance he found more cause for bitterness than pleasure. His wife had died in 1957 and his long partnership with his cousin Pierre Jean-neret was over. Wogensky, his Yugoslavian assistant throughout the 1930s, had left. Resistance to his personality and reputation had robbed him in turn of the League of Nations building, the UN Headquarters in New York and the UNESCO Secretariat in Paris. Worse still, his years of experiment with skyscraper forms had been but a prelude to their universal adoption by men and administrations with no thought for planning, parkland or the excitement of a new machine age. In the strange fashion which often befalls the long-lived, Le Corbusier's pre-dictions and warnings were all coming true without him—and in oddly distorted forms. The world had neither ignored him nor heeded him and the result was much as he and Ozenfant had seen it forty years before —things were perceptibly worse but people were better off—the deluge was still as far away (or as near) as it had appeared in 1923.

In the strangely impotent success of his old age Le Corbusier saw the same imprisoning inertia as he had combated all his life. When he had wanted to build large buildings, when he had wanted to plan cities as an example to the world, the world had turned a deaf ear to his pro-posals; now, when the construction of large buildings and the planning of cities was at his disposal, the real issues had moved elsewhere. Global planning, the pollution of the biosphere, the reduction of architecture to a minor role in the giant pattern of technological evolution—all these things had subtly reduced the significance of the achievements of a life-time. When he died, swimming in the Mediterranean in August 1965, he was still—in his own eyes—slaving over a little-known avant-garde magazine, striving to be noticed, to make it at last.

1 German schools of design in these towns had achieved world fame since the turn of the century—the reason for Jeanneret's visit to Germany

2 *Aujourd'hui*: *art et architecture*, Numéro 51, November 1965, p. 10. Roughly translated, this passage reads: '. . . today are finished childish dreams of a success comparable to that of one or two of the German schools—Vienna, Darmstadt. This is too easy, and I want to take on truth itself. It will make a martyr of me perhaps, even certainly. It is not peace of mind which I look forward to today as I prepare myself for the future. And perhaps still less popular success. . . For myself I shall live, true to my principles, and I shall be content with abuse.'

3 Ibid., p. 14

4 Reyner Banham, *Theory and Design in the First Machine Age*, London, 1960, p. 210

5 Ibid., p. 208

6 *Aujourd'hui*: *art et architecture*, Numéro 51, November 1965, p. 15

7 Reyner Banham, *The Architecture of the well-tempered Environment*, London, 1967, p. 147

8 W. Boesiger, ed., *Le Corbusier 1910–1965*, London and New York, 1967, p. 42

9 P. Boudon, *Pessac de Le Corbusier*, Paris, 1969

10 Reyner Banham, *The Architecture of the well-tempered Environment*, p. 149

11 Ibid.

12 Ibid.

13 Peter Blake, *The Master Builders*, London, 1960, p. 63

14 Quoted in Peter Blake, *The Master Builders*, p. 87

15 Peter Blake, op. cit., p. 119

The Plates

1-4, Headquarters and Refuge for the Salvation Army, Paris (1929-33)

1 The tall entrance porch at the foot of the dormitory block

2 Ground-floor plan showing: 1, entrance hall; 2, main lobby

3 The main entrance from the Rue Cantagrel showing part of circular reception area

4 Glazed south dormitory wall, showing *brise soleil*, applied later, and windows altered to provide opening lights

1

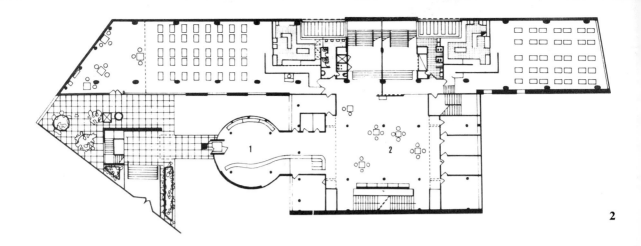

**5-8, Pavillon Suisse (hostel for Swiss students),
Cite Universitaire, Paris (1930-32)**

5 A ground-floor plan of the
Pavillon Suisse showing: 1, dining
room; 2, manager's office; 3, entrance hall

6 The *pilotis* supporting the dormitory block seen from the south-
west

7 The reconstructed-stone wall of
the eastern end of the slab block,
showing how the entire structure
rests upon a reinforced-concrete
base slab—itself supported by
pilotis

8 A view from the south-east
showing blinds in varying positions. The unglazed openings to the
roof terrace can also be seen

5

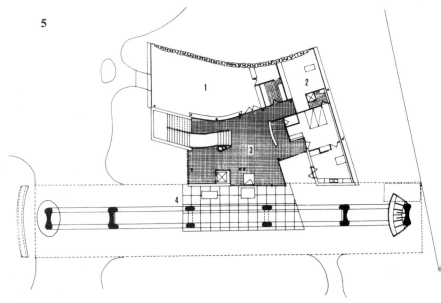

6

**9-11, Pavillon du Bresil (hostel for Brazilian students),
Cite Universitaire, Paris (1957-59)**

9

9 General view from the west

10 The caretaker's entrance

11 The complex column and cross-
beam assembly which replaces the
delicate *pilotis* employed in the
earlier Pavillon Suisse

12-19, The Sarabhai house, Ahmedabad, India (1954-56)

12, 13 First and second floor plans showing: 1, terrace and outdoor rooms; 2, adjoining living area for Mrs Sarabhai's son; 3, garages and servants' quarters; 4, first-floor bedrooms

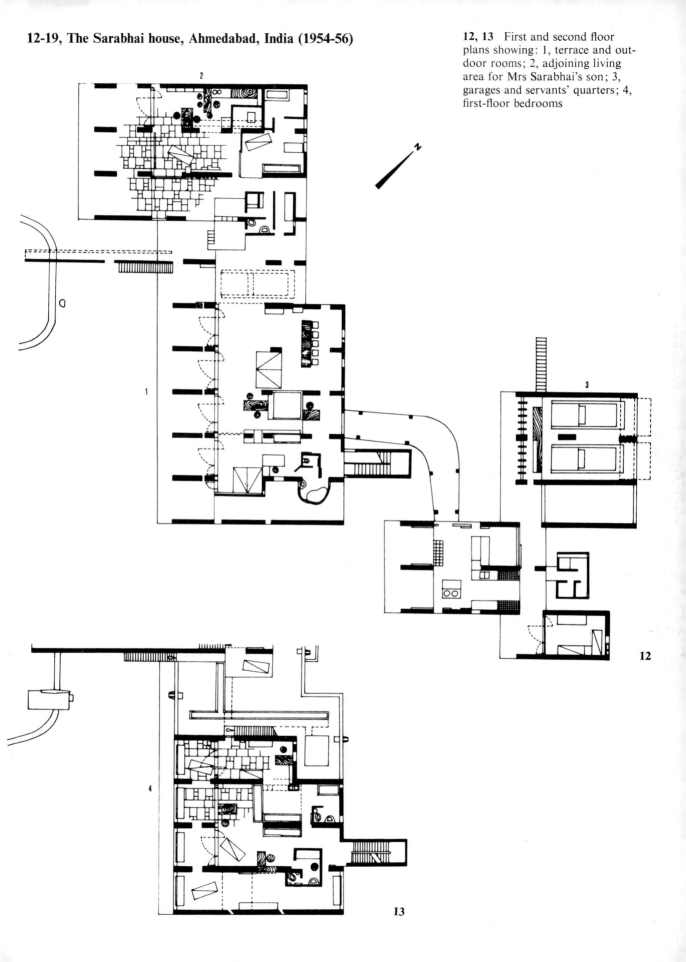

12

13

14 The 'toboggan' which conducts
water to the open-air pool

15 The interior of the ground
floor showing fair-faced brick walls
contrasted with concrete and plastered and painted sections. The
black Madras-stone floor runs
throughout

14

16

16 A rear view of the house showing plants on the roof garden and rainwater gargoyles

17 The tiled vaulted ceiling

18 The semi-outdoor rooms with blinds

19 The living room

17

18

19

20-24, The Shodan house, Ahmedabad, India (1952-56)

20 Façade to the north-east, showing the main entrance with its projecting cantilevered porch

21 Ground-floor plan showing: 1, living room; 2, dining room; 3, kitchen; 4, auxiliary kitchen; 5, servants' quarters; 6, garage

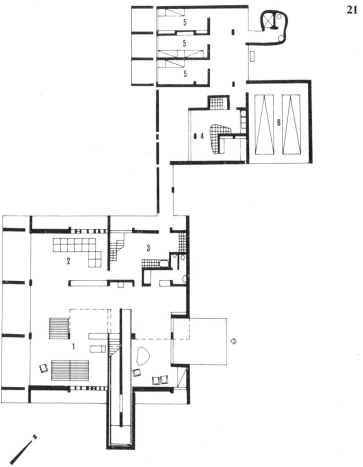

23

22 (*overleaf*) The house from the south-west. The first-floor garden level with circular hole in the roof above it can be clearly seen, as can semi-outdoor rooms on the ground floor

23 The bedrooms on the upper floor

24 Elevation to the west

25-32, Headquarters of the Mill Owners Association of Ahmedabad, India (1954-56)

26 The building seen from across the river

27 Block plan showing: 1, staff houses; 2, roof garden on the main building; 3, offices; 4, parking area

26

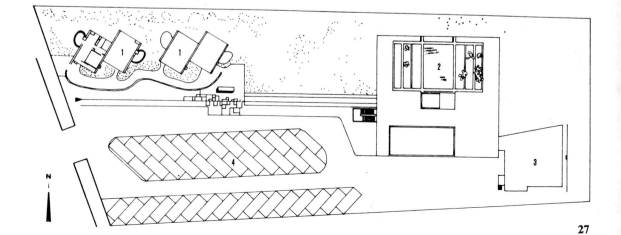

27

28 Plan of principal office floor of the Mill Owners Association building, Ahmedabad: 1, ramp up from car park; 2, reception area; 3, President's office; 4, Vice President's office; 5, secretaries' offices; 6, conference chamber

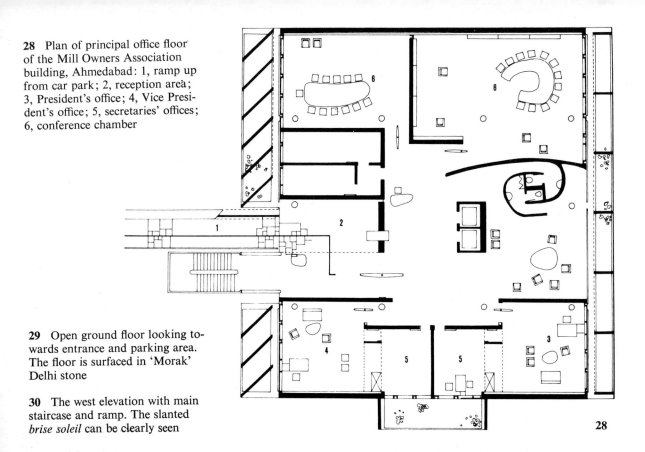

28

29 Open ground floor looking towards entrance and parking area. The floor is surfaced in 'Morak' Delhi stone

30 The west elevation with main staircase and ramp. The slanted *brise soleil* can be clearly seen

29

31 Interior of the conference
room: light is reflected from the
curved concrete roof above, and
sound from the curved, veneered
wall

32 A view across the river through
the *brise soleil*

**33-41, Cultural Centre of Ahmedabad, India:
the Museum (1953-57)**

33 The east elevation showing the extremely short (3.40m.) columns, brick facing, and parapet to roof garden

34 The internal court

33

35

35 The internal court, showing
central pool

36 The short *pilotis* seen from the
first floor within the court

37 The stone-flagged ramp leading
from the court to the first-floor
exhibition area

38 A first-floor exhibition room,
showing stairs from below

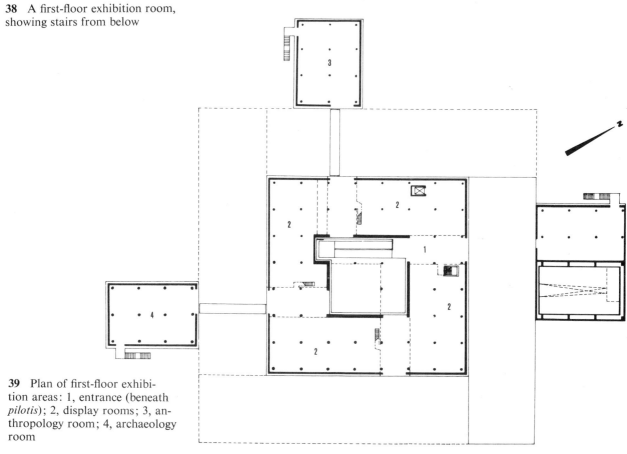

39 Plan of first-floor exhibition areas: 1, entrance (beneath
pilotis); 2, display rooms; 3, an-
thropology room; 4, archaeology
room

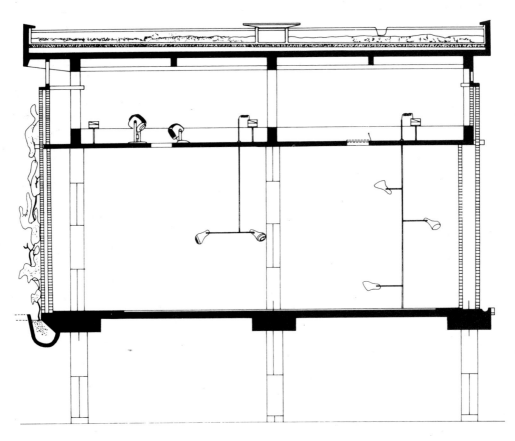

40 Section showing *pilotis*,
large exhibition room with light
fittings, open second-floor area and
roof garden above

41 One of the large exhibition
rooms

42-47, Unité d'habitation, Marseilles (1947-52)

42 Longitudinal section through two storeys of the Marseilles *Unité*, showing the manner in which the full-width apartments with their double-height living rooms overlap, enclosing a single access corridor for every two storeys. This ingenious arrangement speeds lift-service and simplifies the structure by reducing circulation areas to a minimum

43 Section through base *pilotis*, showing drainage and service runs, foundations and cantilevered floor structure

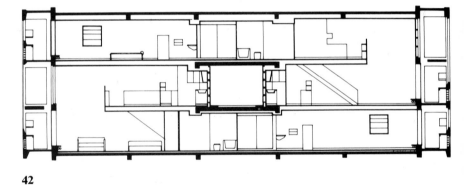

42

44 The south elevation

45 The massive *pilotis* supporting the *Unité*, showing exposed board-marked concrete

46 The open spiral staircase leading to the internal street midway up the building

47 The façade to the east; five storeys up, the row of vertical *brise soleil* reveal the position of the internal street

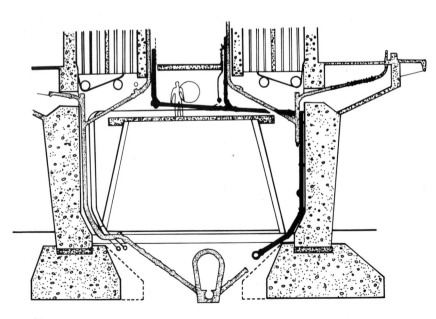

43

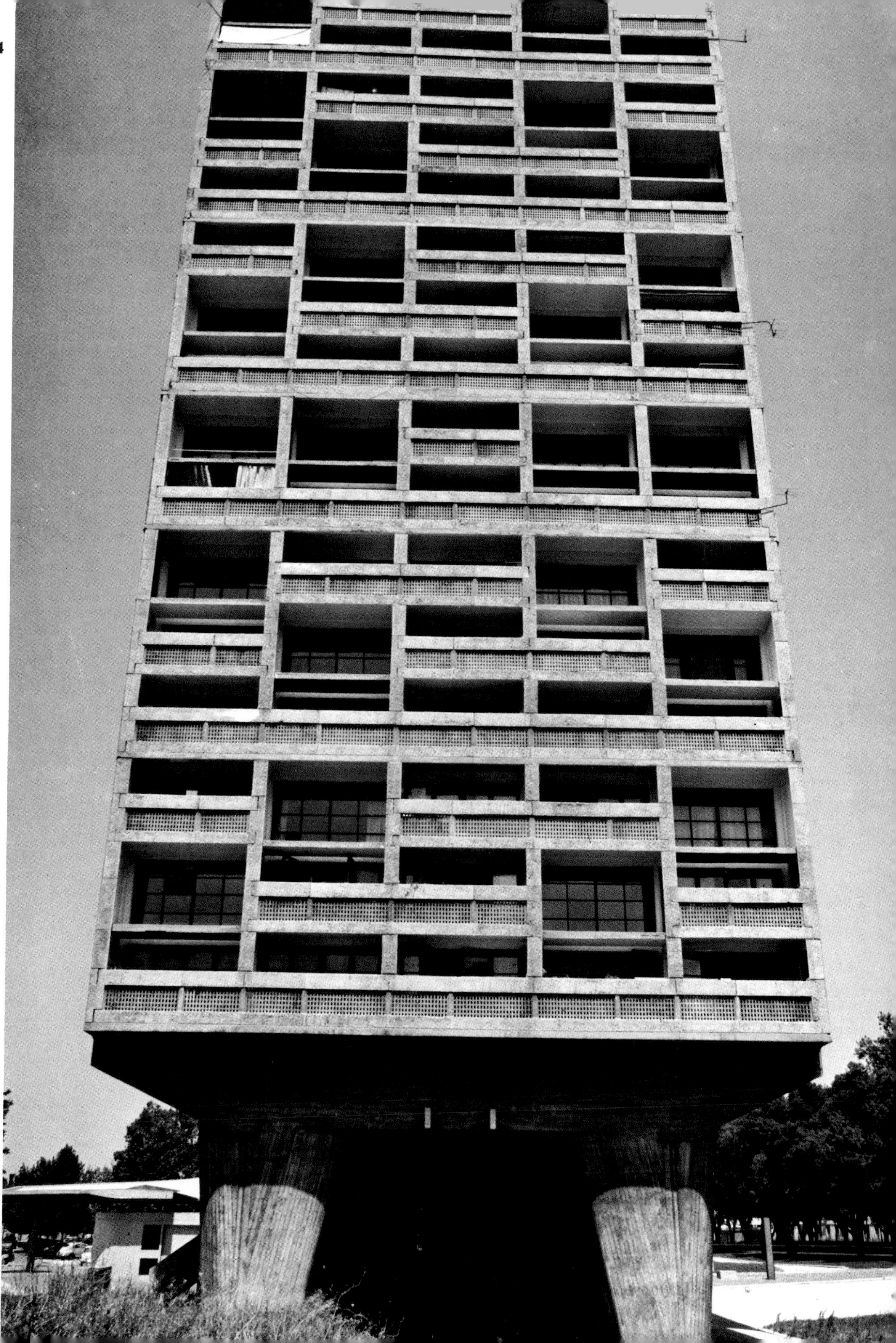

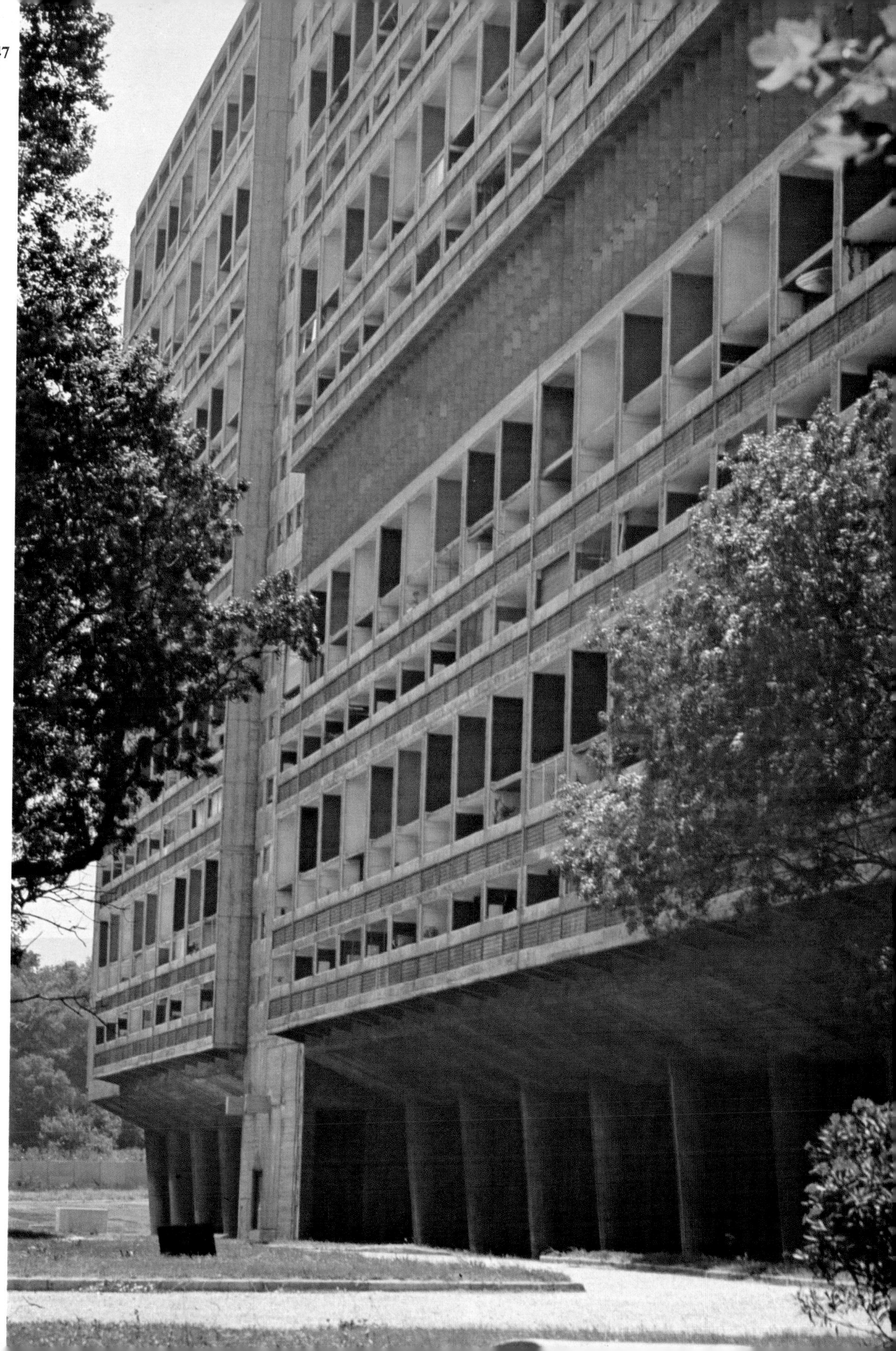

48

49

48 The relief explaining Le Corbusier's Modulor, which the architect had cast into the concrete walls of the *Unité*

49 General view of west elevation

50 A detail of the west elevation showing the use of colour. Compare with plate 47

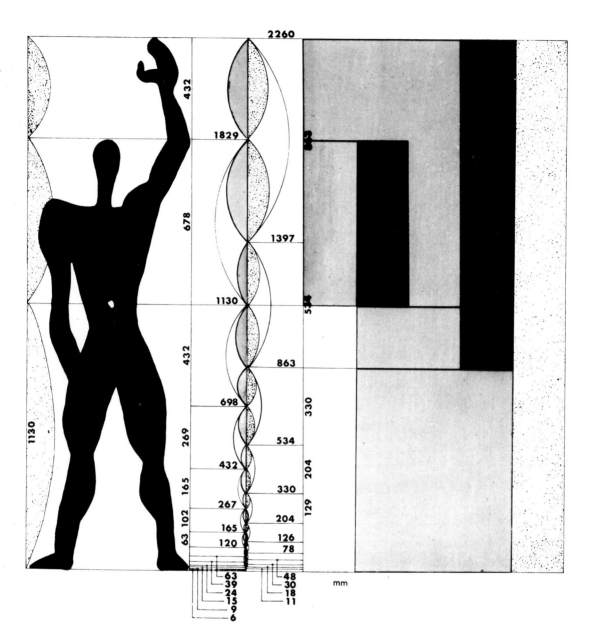

51 Le Corbusier's Modulor. This system of dimensional co-ordination, begun by the architect in 1942, does not consist of multiples and sub-multiples of a basic unit, but rather derives proportions from the ancient 'Golden Section' and the human body from which the 'Golden Section' was itself defined. Modulor, which was first published in 1948, begins with the division of the height of a man into two proportions: the first being the distance from his navel to his upraised hand, and the second from his navel to the soles of his feet. The measurements shown are given in millimetres. From this basic division—which is of course a *proportion* and not a fixed measurement—Le

Corbusier developed a gradually diminishing scale of dimensions. This system, reduced to two rows of ten numbers, was affixed to the wall near the drawing board in each workplace in Le Corbusier's atelier in the Rue de Sèvres. The most famous use of the system was on the Marseilles and Nantes *Unités* where the entire building was dimensioned according to derivatives of the system of proportion described above. Le Corbusier himself records with pride that Albert Einstein—who studied Modulor in 1946—announced that it 'made the bad difficult and the good easy'. It has not however been widely adopted and since Le Corbusier's death seems likely to fall into desuetude

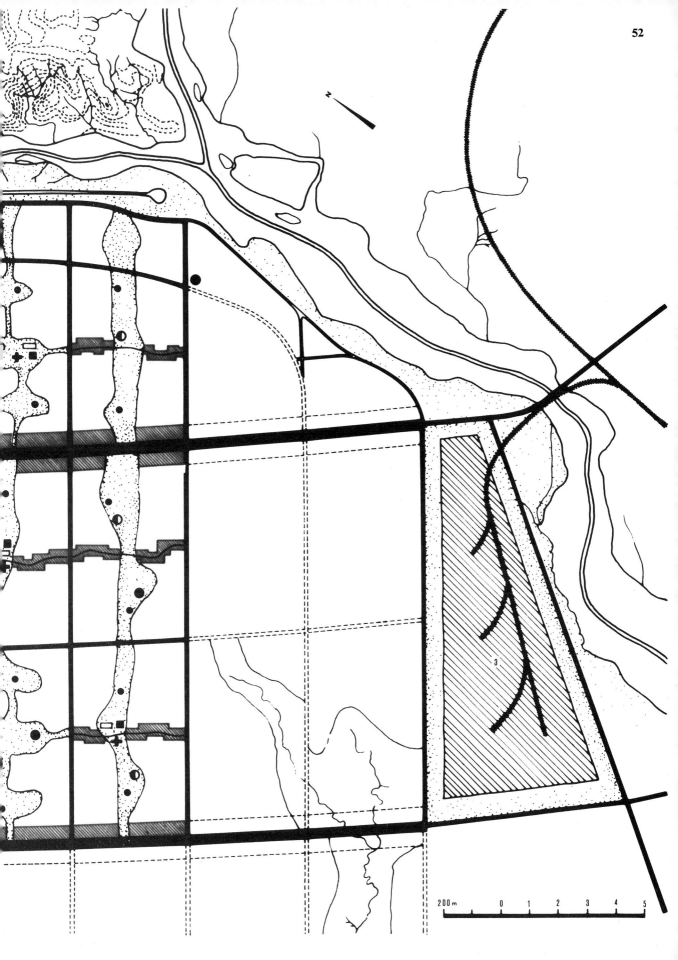

200 m   0   1   2   3   4   5

52, The City of Chandigarh, India. See 53-69

52 *(overleaf)* Chandigarh, master plan: 1, government and administrative offices; 2, business centre; 3, industrial area; O, schools; +, hospitals; □, community centres

53-56, The Courts of Justice, Chandigarh (1951-56)

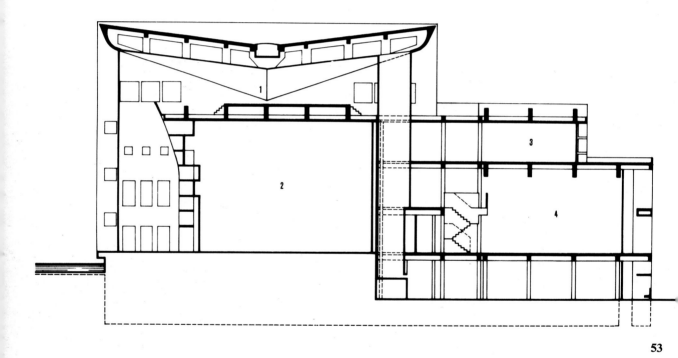

53

53 Section showing: 1, terrace beneath umbrella roof; 2, courtroom; 3, library; 4, restaurant

54 The main entrance to the Courts of Justice, showing the enormous scale of the rendered and painted columns dwarfing the rows of flower pots

55 The main elevation of the Courts of Justice, showing characteristic use of bright colours

56 Rear elevation, facing south-
east

57-61, The Secretariat, Chandigarh (1952-58)

Overleaf

57 The Secretariat (left) and the Palace of Assembly, seen across the 'Boulevard des Eaux' from the Courts of Justice

58 North-east elevation of the Secretariat

59 Part of the roof garden of the
Secretariat

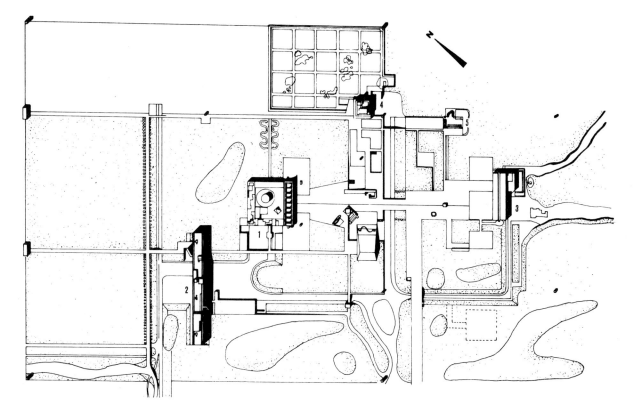

60 Plan of the Capitol at
Chandigarh showing: 1, Palace of
Assembly; 2, Secretariat (admin-
istration building); 3, Courts of
Justice; 4, Governor's residence;
5, Monument of the Open Hand

61 Part elevation of the Secretariat, showing Ministers' rooms
shielded by *brise soleil* with narrow
'ventilators' behind

62-69, The Palace of Assembly, Chandigarh (1953-60)

62 (*overleaf*) General view of the Palace of Assembly

63, 64 Section and elevation of the Palace of Assembly showing: 1, free-standing portico, from the steps of which the foothills of the Himalaya are visible; 2, Assembly Hall; 3, offices

65 Raised footways connecting the Palace of Assembly with other Capitol buildings; there are no staircases within the building itself, only concrete ramps

66 The obliquely cut off aluminium roof to the Assembly Hall

67 Interior of the Assembly Hall, showing circular form and elaborate acoustic treatment

68 Detail of the main portico facing south-east

69 The Palace of Assembly seen through the portico of the Courts of Justice

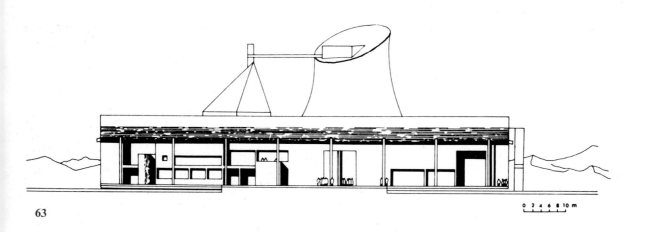

63

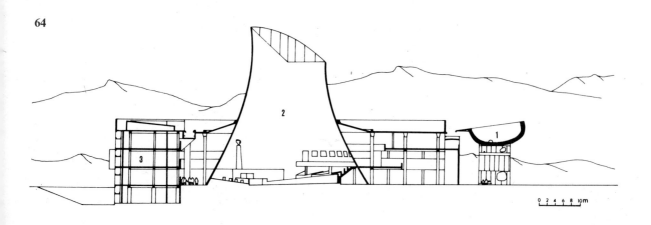

64

66

65

67

70-79, Chapel at Ronchamp, Vosges, France (1950-53)

70 The enamelled centre-hung processional door

71 Ronchamp from the south-east, showing fair-faced concrete roof and rendered walls with window openings

72 The north elevation

73 Site plan of the Ronchamp chapel, showing basic masonry structure in relation to pilgrims' hostel (bottom left) and pyramid (bottom right)

74 Tower with windows, and twin gargoyle to discharge rainwater from main roof; part of the aluminium cladding of the upper roof membrane can also be seen

75 The interior of the tower

76 The altar at the foot of the tower

72

73

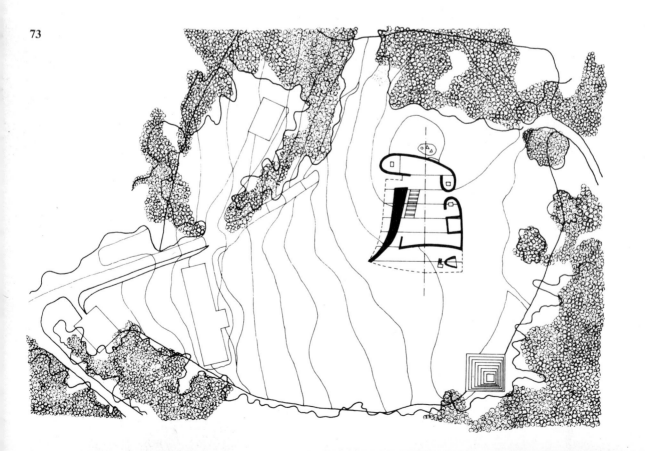

74

77 Interior of the chapel looking east

78 Axonometric drawing of the chapel showing modular wall openings

79 Interior view showing coloured glass in the wall openings and thickness of walls

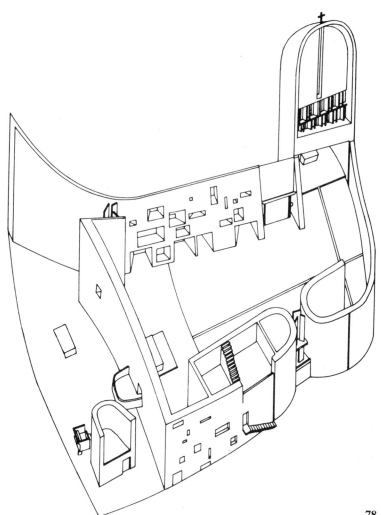

78

**80-89, Monastery of La Tourette,
near Lyons, France (1956-60)**

80 A view of La Tourette from the north-east showing the battery of light-cannons set into the roof of the side chapel

81 A closer view showing the undulating glazing of the lower storeys, with fixed lights set between thin concrete mullions at varying intervals

82 The south elevation, showing double row of monks' cells above communal rooms

83 The rough-cast concrete wall of the church with, in the foreground, light-cannons protruding from the roof of the sunken chapel

84 The sunken side-chapel following the slope of the ground. As at Ronchamp bright primary colours are used sparingly

82

85

85 The inner court

86 The glazed cloister flanking the
inner court

87 Plan of the upper level at
La Tourette showing: 1, church;
2, monks' cells

86

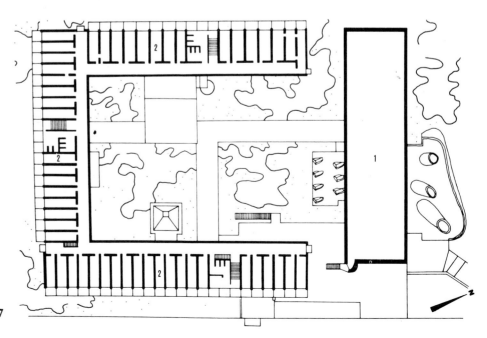

87

88 Interior of the church with
sunken side-chapel beyond

89 The altar of the side-chapel

90-96, Visual Arts Center, Harvard University, Cambridge, Mass. (1961-64)

92

90

90 The ramp entry from the east

91 General arrangement, showing: 1, exhibition space; 2, entrance from elevated walkway; 3, studio

92 Elevation to the east showing ramp access to second-floor level and slanted *brise soleil*

93 Ramp access to the west. To the left can be seen part of the Georgian-style Fogg Museum

94 Access ramp and slanted *brise soleil*

95 The ramp passing through the building with plate glass windows on either side

96 Ramp access to the west side, with service block on the right

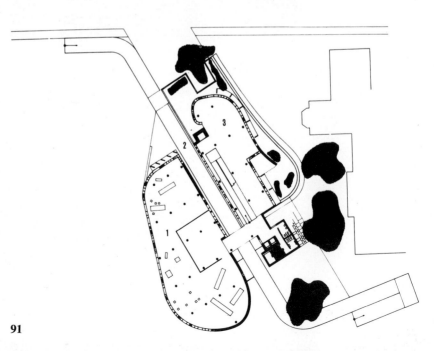

91

View of Manhattan: the simultaneous achievement in New York of Le Corbusier's wildest dreams and fears. 'The skyscrapers are too small,' he observed on the occasion of his first visit, 'and there is too much space between them.'

Notes on the plates

1-4
Headquarters and Refuge for the Salvation Army, Paris (1929–33)

At the time of commissioning this building was the largest ever tackled by Le Corbusier and certainly the most prestigious. The site was long and narrow offering only a short, oblique frontage to the Rue Cantagrel: plans to develop a further series of large blocks on an adjoining site to the north failed to materialize. Le Corbusier arranged the dormitory accommodation for the refuge in a tall slab block along the north perimeter of the site with an auditorium and other facilities at its foot. The block itself featured an entirely glazed wall to the south whose enormous heat gain and loss was to have been offset by a system of ventilation ('la respiration exacte'), and a type of temperature-controlled double glazing ('le mur neutralisant'), capable of maintaining a constant 18°C in all weathers whilst retaining the benefits of maximum sunlight for the 'six hundred poor souls' who would live there.

The triumphant opening in December 1933 with the building basking in winter sunlight and warm as toast was soon to give way to a tropical nightmare at the height of the summer. Severe economies during construction—largely brought on by the unstable nature of the subsoil and corresponding need for piling—had robbed the project of its double glazing and the cooling plant for the 'respiration exacte'. The sealed, single-glazed south wall became a minor scandal and the city authorities insisted on the fitting of additional screening. Some years later (after bomb damage) the building was fitted with *brise soleil* in a further effort to bring the temperature in the dormitories under control.

5-8
Pavillon Suisse (hostel for Swiss students), Cité Universitaire, Paris (1930–32)

Commissioned after the scandal of the League of Nations competition, which Le Corbusier and Pierre Jeanneret won in 1927 but were refused permission to proceed with, the Pavillon Suisse was financed by a federation of Swiss universities at a final cost of only three million francs—half the figure originally agreed. The building itself, despite its small size, has exerted an enormous influence on the development of the modern movement since its completion.

Consisting of a precise four-storey slab, free-standing and raised on *pilotis* to provide one further storey, the structure is flanked to the north by a curved staircase tower in reconstructed stone and glass bricks. A further low block echoes the curve of the staircase wall in random rubble, capped by a white-painted fascia and glazed from wall to ceiling to the west. The brown-painted, steel-framed glazing on the south wall is fitted with vertical roller blinds in aluminium in an effort to offset the kind of heat-gain that proved so troublesome in the Salvation Army building. A consequence of the light concrete-framed structure was a particularly poor sound-reduction performance between student rooms. Efforts were made to conquer this by means of suspended lead sheets and discrete outer skins, but with little effect. Like many famous modern buildings the Pavillon Suisse solves some problems extremely well—but at the expense of a cure being found for others.

9-11
Pavillon du Brésil (hostel for Brazilian students), Cité Universitaire, Paris, (1957–59)

Thirty years after designing the Pavillon Suisse, Le Corbusier supervised the construction of one of its neighbours—the Brazilian Pavilion. This squat, heavy building, lacking the purity and grace of its predecessor, was allegedly designed by Lucio Costa, and the Corbusian apologists generally explain away its appearance on these grounds. In some ways this building marks an uneasy mixture of the massive *béton brut* structure of the *Unités* with some feeble echoes of the architect's 'Cartesian' period; despite sharing the same general format as that of its predecessor (apart from its orientation which is more conventional), it utterly fails to achieve distinction. The random stone walling used occasionally on the single-storey areas is particularly unimpressive. As Reyner Banham notes of another building, it has the quality of 'a surrealist quotation from another period.'

12–19
The Sarabhai house,
Ahmedabad, India (1954–56)

Almost completely concealed by vegetation, the Sarabhai house is constructed of red brick and rough-cast concrete. The vaulted structure (faced with clay tiles), recalls the contemporaneous Maison Jaoul at Neuilly-sur-Seine, whilst the extraordinary open form of the building, which allows air to pass freely from one side to the other, reflects Le Corbusier's deep study of the needs of housing in an Indian climate. The doors which close off the outside are designed to be used as variable reflectors which, in conjunction with the *brise soleil*, can modulate the amount of light and air entering the house. The roof has a garden extending over its full area and the flooring in dark Madras stone continues out into the area immediately surrounding the house.

20–24
The Shodan house,
Ahmedabad, India (1952–56)

The coarse concrete of which this house is constructed reveals much patching and filling consequent upon the concrete having adhered to the rough formwork. Effectively built on two storeys, connected by a ramp, the house also features a flat, punctured roof which floats above the main structure on columns—thus permitting free air passage between the elements of the house. Built with separate servants' quarters, the house possesses a stark and military quality which is relieved by the same brightly coloured panels and fabrics as in the Sarabhai house.

25–32
Headquarters of the
Mill Owners Association
of Ahmedabad, India
(1954–56)

More than most of Le Corbusier's Indian buildings the Mill Owners Association headquarters reveals its origins in the architect's 'Domino' structure of 1914. In Europe the glass-walled or open-sided dwelling proved difficult to develop successfully for climatic, population-density and acoustic reasons; forty years later the architect was able to execute designs using this principle in India. Here the structure is strongly disciplined and oriented in accordance with the prevailing wind direction. Both east and west façades have *brise soleil* and adjustable blinds; the roof garden extends over the whole area of the building.

From the lowest level to the proof two lifts serve all floors. A long ramp provides pedestrian access from the parking area to the main office floor. The structure consists of fair-faced brick on the north and south façades, whilst the east and west elevations are of rough-cast concrete. The *brise soleil* are clad in wood and some of the internal walls in sheet metal.

33–41
Cultural Centre of Ahmedabad, India: the Museum (1953–57)

Based loosely on Le Corbusier's 'Museum of unlimited extension' project of 1939, which featured a square spiral using standardized structural elements, the Ahmedabad museum stands upon *pilotis* at 7 metre centres and encloses an open court from which access to the exhibition rooms is gained. The main level is entered through a series of squares (with sides of 14 metres) arranged in a spiral shape. The roof garden contains forty-five pools, each fifty square metres in area and surrounded with vegetation, which serve to create a cool atmosphere, particularly in the evening when the building is generally used. The concrete-framed building is faced in uncoursed brickwork both inside and outside the court. Internally the walls are plastered. As with the original 1939 design the size of the museum is not limited to its present configuration but can be increased by the addition of standard structural units.

42–47
Unité d'habitation, Marseilles (1947–52)

After the abandonment of Le Corbusier's master plan for Saint-Dié, the *Unité* at Marseilles became his most important post-war commission in France. Planned to house 1,600 persons from the bombed out port area, the *Unité* was to have been the first of four similar structures on neighbouring sites. In the event the scandals surrounding this first building—which was only completed through the uncompromising support given to Le Corbusier by the then Minister of Reconstruction, M. Claudius-Petit—wrecked any chances of further developments in the Marseilles area.

The building, aligned on a north-south axis, is raised twenty-three feet above ground level on *pilotis*, contains one 'internal street' with shops, and 337 transverse apartments, each running the full width of the building. They are scaled to accommodate varying sizes of family—from single persons to those with up to five children. The east-west orientation of the apartments allows through ventilation, and the heavily sculptured roof level houses a small school, a gymnasium and a meeting hall—as well as gardens and terraces.

48–51
Unité d'habitation, West Berlin (1956–57)

Some thirty years after the famous *Werkbund* exhibition at the Weissenhofsiedlung in Stuttgart, the West German government resolved to carry out a similar project—inviting many famous architects to take part—for the redevelopment of the Tiergarten Park in West Berlin. The exhibition, called Interbau, took place in 1957. As on the earlier occasion Le Corbusier was invited, but instead of designing individual houses he proposed a third *Unité* as his contribution. The site allocated to him was adjacent to the still extant stadium built under the Nazi government for the 1936 Olympic Games.

The Berlin *Unité* is considerably larger than that of Marseilles, comprising 400 apartments, but difficulties with the Berlin authorities led to the architect repudiating the building before its completion. The chief cause of dispute was the refusal of the authorities to accept the 226 cm. modular ceiling height according to which the *Unités* at both Marseilles and Nantes-Rezé had been built. In consequence of the intransigence of both parties the windows were all modified to fit a higher ceiling, with the result that the proportions of the whole were destroyed. Similarly the use of colour, carefully controlled at Marseilles (see pl. 47) is here used rigidly over the whole façade (pl. 50).

52
The City of Chandigarh,
Punjab, India
(see also 53–69)

This, the major project of Le Corbusier's last years, began in 1950 with the decision of the Indian government to construct a new regional capital for the Punjab—the former capital Lahore having been ceded to Pakistan at the time of the partition of 1947. Although responsible for the master plan of the city (which will house 500,000 persons after the completion of the first two phases of its construction), and appointed 'advisor' on all matters connected with its future development, Le Corbusier designed only the capitol in detail, distributing much of the additional work to other modern architects of his choice.

Between 1951 and 1954 two British members of the Congrès International d'Architecture Moderne (CIAM), Jane Drew and Maxwell Fry, worked on the project, concentrating on the design of housing. The capitol is in the tradition of Le Corbusier's earlier town-planning projects culminating in the abortive Saint-Dié master plan, although at Chandigarh all the buildings are official. They comprise: an assembly building, the parliament; an 800-foot long secretariat, eight storeys high; a small governor's palace; the Courts of Justice—all interrelated by careful landscaping, and all dominated by the 'Monument of the Open Hand' —a gigantic sculptural symbol of the aspirations embodied in the design.

The expansive and diffused character of the capital city which will emerge derives partly from the preferences of the British educated administrators in the Indian government, with whom Le Corbusier was obliged to negotiate. An aspect of their influence is also to be seen in the housing which is arranged in thirteen descending orders of magnificence—from prince down to peasant.

Part of the landscaping at Chandigarh called for the damming of a small river to produce the 'Boulevard des Eaux', one of a number of lakes intended to modulate the micro-climate of the region as well as provide dramatic vistas of the capitol buildings. The curving esplanade which crowns the dam retaining the 'Boulevard des Eaux' is over twenty-four metres wide and four kilometres in length. It was completed in 1955. The eventual form of Chandigarh—following the death of Le Corbusier in 1965—has become once again problematical, and like the similarly spacious but larger Brasilia it has already provoked much criticism on the grounds of grandiloquence and impractical scale. The robust quality of the buildings at Chandigarh—and the architect's wise use of native Indian constructional practice wherever possible—may save the massive monuments to his genius from the sad fate of the great buildings of Brasilia—doomed by poor workmanship and inadequate maintenance to a rapid decline during their first decade of life. Nonetheless the quality of urban environment which eventually emerges in the new capital of the Punjab will, almost certainly, turn out to be rather different from that envisaged by the architect.

53–56
The Courts of Justice,
Chandigarh (1951–56)

In use since 1956, the Courts of Justice was the first major capitol building to be completed at Chandigarh. It is an enormous vaulted structure capped by a concrete roof umbrella that shelters a four-storey, unwalled entrance lobby lined with concrete ramps and topped by arches. To both sides of this lobby are courtrooms on several levels—all shielded by an irregular array of *brise soleil* on the principal (north-west) elevation. The three main columns dividing the entrance are cement rendered and painted respectively green, yellow and a pinkish red. Both left and right flanking walls are painted black. Inside the courtrooms, whose walls are cast in concrete, necessary sound-absorption is achieved by means of over 7,000 square feet of tapestry woven in five months by Kashmiri craftsmen according to the architect's own designs. The effect of these when hung in the timeless gloom of the enormous, non air-conditioned interiors, is particularly impressive. Unexpected heat build-up at the foot of the giant building led to the later addition of a covered way along the main façade to the right of the entrance arches.

57–61
The Secretariat, Chandigarh (1952–58)

Similar in its general appearance to the Marseilles *Unité*, the Secretariat with its 800-foot elevations facing north-west and south-east presents a strongly articulated façade in each direction. Projections, recesses, stair towers, changes in pattern are all derived from the 'Modulor' and conspire to give the building a restless and dynamic air which belies its vast bulk and horizontal form.

Housing three thousand employees, the building was the second major capitol structure to be completed, providing offices for Punjabi State Ministers and their agencies. Climatic control in the Secretariat, with its enormous bands of windows, is aided by the provision of full-height adjustable sheet-metal 'ventilators' set behind copper mosquito-netting.

62–69
The Palace of Assembly, Chandigarh (1953–60)

The fourth capitol building to be completed at Chandigarh, the Palace of Assembly is in many ways the most impressive. Based on an almost square plan, the structure incorporates an enormous frustum-shaped assembly hall passing through several floors and rising above the roof level. The hyperbolic shell of the assembly hall is only 150 mm. thick and is a correspondingly light and cheap structure closely resembling the cooling towers used at power stations or in industrial facilities where enormous heat-exchanging potential is required. In the case of the Assembly Hall the dubious acoustics resulting from this form are modulated by sound-absorbent panels in bright colours and random curvilinear shapes suspended from the walls of the cone. The construction of the complete building is *in-situ* reinforced concrete—as in all the other capitol buildings—although entirely different techniques are used for the trabeated structure surrounding the Assembly Hall.

70–79
Chapel at Ronchamp, Vosges, France (1950–53)

Probably Le Corbusier's most famous building, this chapel was built to replace an earlier building destroyed during the Second World War. Much of the stone used in the old chapel has been re-used in the new design—particularly in the enormous battered walls.

The whole conception of Ronchamp is dominated by the reverse-curved, asymmetrical roof—itself cast in two separate membranes separated by a space of about seven feet. This heavy roof is supported above the massive walls by short reinforced-concrete columns which stiffen the 'Gunnite' coated masonry walls and relieve them of much of the load that they apparently carry. At the same time the enormous thickness and curvilinear plan-form of the masonry contributes to its stability.

The floor of the chapel is finished in cement paving sized in panels according to the 'Modulor' and separated by permanent shuttering in the form of battens. The slope towards the altar follows the natural line of the site.

The towers are constructed in masonry, capped with concrete domes and spray-rendered, as are all the main vertical surfaces.

Daylighting is based upon a system of openings penetrating the thick masonry walls and glazed near the outer surface in plain and coloured glass. The doors of the chapel are particularly remarkable, the main processional one is centre pivoted and covered on each face with eight panels of sheet steel enamelled in primary colours. The door opening eastward onto the podium for open-air services is of cast concrete with bronze furniture.

80–89
Monastery of La Tourette, near Lyons (1956–60)

Commissioned at the instigation of Reverend Father Couturier, the monastery of La Tourette is sited on the slope of a hill at Eveux-sur-Arbresle, near Lyons. Built in the form of a hollow rectangle, the reinforced-concrete structure provides sleeping accommodation for one hundred students and teachers, study rooms, a workshop, recreation room, a library and a refectory. One whole side of the block is a church with a partly underground chapel flanking it. The pronounced slope of the site prevented the traditional cloister form except around the interior of the unpaved central court. The flat concrete columns which support the south elevation overlooking the valley rest on piles, and the site itself is left unterraced between them so that the unkempt natural *pelouse* flows under and around the building on all sides.

The upper storey—devoted on three sides to the cells of the monks, whose open balconies, isolated one from another, form the familiar *brise soleil* effect—was according to Le Corbusier designed first with the remaining communal accommodation fitted in beneath them.

90–96
Visual Arts Center, Harvard University, Cambridge, Mass. (1961–64)

This building, Le Corbusier's first and only one in the United States, straddles an elevated walkway and is set obliquely between two of the traditional buildings of the Harvard University campus. Although designed by Le Corbusier, construction was supervised by José Luis Sert, the famous Spanish architect. The purpose of the Center, which is open to all students, is to promote the integration of intellectual and craft activities—an aim to which the architect himself attached the greatest importance.

The construction is of glass and concrete, and the main entrance, from the elevated walkway, is at second-floor level. Accommodation comprises an entrance hall, reception room, lecture room, studio, auditorium, offices, exhibition space and a roof garden.

Chronological list: projects and events

1887 Born 6 October at La Chaux-de-Fonds, Switzerland
1900 Enrols as apprentice-engraver at La Chaux-de-Fonds School of Art
1905 Designs first house at La Chaux-de-Fonds
1908 Works with Auguste Perret in Paris
1911 Works with Peter Behrens in Germany
1914 Jeanneret develops 'Domino' frame housing project
1916 Villa Schwob, La Chaux-de-Fonds
1918 Jeanneret in Paris
1920 Founds magazine *L'Esprit Nouveau* with the painter Ozenfant; first adopts the pseudonym 'Le Corbusier'
1922 Opens atelier at 35 Rue de Sèvres, Paris, with his cousin Pierre Jeanneret. City for three million inhabitants (project); 'Citrohan' (Citroen) housing for mass production (project)
1923 Publication of *Vers une Architecture*
1925 Break up of partnership with Ozenfant; Pavillon de l'Esprit Nouveau at the International Exhibition of Decorative Arts, Paris; house for parents at Vevey, Lake Geneva; Voisin Plan for Paris (project); housing at Pessac, Bordeaux
1926 'Five Points of Modern Architecture'
1927 Villa Garches, near Paris; Palace of the League of Nations Competition entry; two prototype houses for the Weissenhofsiedlung, Stuttgart
1928 First Congress of Congrès International d'Architecture Moderne (CIAM), La Sarraz, Switzerland; Villa at Carthage, Tunisia
1929 Design for Centrosoyus, Moscow
1930 Le Corbusier becomes a French citizen
1931 Completion of 'Les Heures Claires' at Poissy; completion of Salvation Army building, Paris; Palace of the Soviets, Moscow (project)
1932 Completion of Pavillon Suisse, Cité Universitaire, Paris
1933 Fourth Congress of CIAM at Athens; Athens Charter; apartment house in Algiers with *brise soleil* (project)

1935 First visit to USA

1936 Begins collaboration over Ministry of Education building, Rio de Janeiro, Argentina; 'Ilôt Insalubre', No. 6: slum clearance project, Paris

1937 The Cartesian Skyscraper (project)

1938 Le Quartier de la Marine, Algiers, planning project

1939 Ideal Home Exhibition, London

1942 Algiers master plan (project)

1945 Town plan for Saint-Dié (project)

1947 Collaboration over United Nations Building, New York

1951 Planning of Chandigarh begins

1952 Completion of *Unité d'habitation* at Marseilles

1954 Completion of Chapel at Notre Dame-du-Haut, Ronchamp

1956 Courts of Justice, Chandigarh completed; Villa Sarabhai and Villa Shodan at Ahmedabad completed

1957 *Unité d'habitation* at Nantes-Rezé completed; *Unité d'habitation* at Berlin completed

1959 Monastery of La Tourette completed; Pavillon du Brésil, Cité Universitaire, Paris; Museum at Tokyo

1960 *Unités d'habitation* at Briey-en-Forêt

1963 Computer Centre for Olivetti, Milan

1964 Visual Arts Center, Cambridge, Mass.

1965 Maison des Jeunes et de la culture, Firminy, France; French Embassy for Brasilia (project); Hospital at Venice (project)

1965 27 August, Le Corbusier dies

1967 Completion of Exhibition Centre at Zurich

Select bibliography

Books by Le Corbusier
Vers une Architecture, Paris, 1923 (Editions Crès), republished 1959 (Editions Vincent, Fréal); published in English, trans. Frederick Etchells, as *Towards a New Architecture*, London, 1959
Propos d'Urbanisme, Paris, 1946; published in English, trans. Clive Entwistle, as *Concerning Town Planning*, London, 1948

Books and articles on Le Corbusier
Peter Blake, *The Master Builders*, London, 1960
W. Boesiger, ed., *Le Corbusier: The Complete Architectural Works*, 7 vols, London and New York, 1966: I, 1910–1929; II, 1929–1934; III, 1934–1938 (ed. Max Bill); IV, 1938–1946; V, 1946–1952; VI, 1952–1957; VII, 1957–1965;
Le Corbusier 1910-1965, London and New York, 1967
Philippe Boudon, *Pessac de Le Corbusier*, Paris, 1969
Françoise Choay, *Le Corbusier*, New York, 1960
Maximilien Gauthier, *Le Corbusier, or the architect in the service of man*, Paris, 1944, and New York, 1945
Siegfried Giedion, 'Le Corbusier et l'architecture contemporaine', *Cahiers d'Art*, V, pp. 204–15

Special issues of journals devoted to Le Corbusier
Architecture d'aujourd'hui: on Le Corbusier and Pierre Jeanneret, May 1933; 60th birthday issue, April 1948
Aujourd'hui: art and architecture, Numéro 51, November 1965

Index

135